Strategies & Relationships

Strategies and Relationships in Business Management and Development: Beyond Step by Step into the Heart of Building an Enterprise

By José Sosa

Printed in the United States of America

ISBN: 978-1-71667-266-8

Graphics by: Elvis Salic www.elvissalic.com

Dedication

This book is dedicated to Celenia Pineda-Sosa, my wife and
Cruzelina Sosa, my mother. Thank you for making me believe
that anything is possible.

Contents

Contents

Preface: The Mindsets

I own a barbershop in the entertainment capital of the world. I do not advertise, but I have a 3-month waiting list for guests seeking to utilize the services I provide. With the onset of COVID-19, guests are able to get appointments sometimes within a day of booking. My workload has not decreased, and neither has my bottom line. Everything has slowed down in the barbershop world. Still, my shop is clocking 30% new clients per week. Once everything gets back to normal, there will be more clients than we can handle.

I have also started another business that provides Designs and Solutions for Small Businesses. People always asked me, "Who manages your social media and your logo?" A solid rule of business development is to pay attention to what friends, clients, and others ask you about. This signals your expertise and the information customers may be willing to pay you for.

Organic reach is my chosen marketing tool. We did not reinvent the wheel, but we connected intentionally with people. I wrote a blog with SEO. I put out content for free. I launched the blog and received immediate responses of nearly 800 per day in 8 days. In 2 months, we have secured 20 invoices.

My mindset is about creating freedom though my evolution was a long time coming. I have been successful in cutting hair, but my definition of success has changed. In the beginning, the drive for success was financially measured. Today, the definition of success is freedom measure in the time I own to do what I want to do. I went on 42 trips last year, enjoying something more valuable than money: time. I realize that I am still trading time for money in my business. I want to begin to trade ideas for money. I want to leverage freedom and reclaim my time while increasing the money. I want that for all my family. The grind is not for the money; it is for balance. If I am spending time behind the chair for 12–14 hours per day, I don't have time with my family, but I am also out of balance. Balance is taking care of myself holistically. That means providing appropriate time for all areas of my life that are important to me. It also means prioritizing the most important things in my life. Consider that no matter how much money you make, being tethered to a chair feels like prison.

Now, I time myself in everything that I do. What I am selling is not a commodity; I am selling a premium service done right the first time. This is true in my barbershop as well as my design business. It may seem expensive to some, but our designs are scalable and responsive. You can put our graphics on a website or blow it up and put it on a plane.

Often, you spend your adult life looking for more money. When you get the money, you realize that time is more valuable. Taking an approach to reclaim your time is a much more sustainable approach. I am 15 years into my profession. I wish I had understood reclaiming time at year 5. My situation would be different now. I believe I would have more of my own time and more money as well.

Strategies vs Relationships

While developing the mindsets between strategies and relationships, I noticed similarities; but most importantly, I noticed key differences. I noticed that if you have a strategic mindset, the relationship will suffer. The same goes with having a relationship mindset; the strategy will suffer. Understanding the differences between both has helped me become successful. Understanding the differences has allowed me to develop a strong business acumen.

Strategy is about making fewer mistakes. You must know the rules of the game before you can break them. Strategy details the rules of the game. In my barbershop, the primary strategy is to provide the best haircut. Without that, your clients will go elsewhere.

Relationships are about balancing your time. If you sleep for 8 hours and engage in life for another 8, what do you do with the work in the remaining 8 hours? Your business will run without you present because of the relationships you create. That is the goal. If you must work 12-hour days until you retire, that's a jail sentence. You want to work when you want and as you want. It is about finding the sweet spot in your business—moving from worker to manager and from manager to owner. When it is done correctly, you don't have to watch to make sure partners are doing what they should be doing. You can trust, engage, and ensure that people are happy. They are people you want to golf with, invite to birthday parties, and spend time with. Work is a part of the equation, but life is balancing all of the activities to your enjoyment.

I have serviced many millionaires in my career. Each of them still goes to work each day. They get up five days per week and go to their private gym, their office, and return home in the evenings. They have the money to retire by typical standards, but they find their enjoyment in the balance they have created.

The Gain

Every book that I have read bring you to the point of developing the business and the hard work. They emphasize the work and the investment. This text will lay emphasis on your why.

A great ad states who they are, what they sell, and why they sell. The amazing ads lead with the why. The process of that is what you will gain from this text. This provides a well-rounded view of what you need to achieve your definition of success.

Your definitions will change based on your experience. When you see money, time, wealth, success, and those experiences for yourself, your perception of them changes. It is like Jay-Z found in the development of the 4:44 album. I am certain that he found a blueprint through his journey through the music business. I am sure there was a great deal of trial and error. He almost lost all that he thought he was working for. He arrived at a point to realize what really mattered and what was noise. He shared his wisdom in the album.

I wish I had recognized it earlier, but I am still excited. The author of Good to Great interviewed self-made billionaires around the world, asking them the same questions. The responses were compiled in a second book. He released one of the questions. It asked, "What is the one thing you would do over if you could?" Each one of them answered the same.

"Take more risks." That stuck with me. I had always thought that I needed to trade my time for money. I learned the value of time and realized that I could do something different. I am happy that I learned it later. If not, I would have been working for more money. Now, I am working as if each new venture is a passion project. I am excited to create a business that connects with value for each of my clients.

I once forgot to send an invoice to one of my clients because there was a great deal of passion and activity around what I was doing. The client came to me and reminded me that they needed to pay. I would not have known until my accountant or CFO reviewed the books at the end of the year. This would not have been the focus back when I started. Delayed gratification is the best gratification. You can win in the immediate term, but if you wait until the timing is best, you will enjoy life more. I don't stress over time anymore. Everything in my world is aligned for my benefit. I have learned to trust that reality. The proof for me is my experience of success.

The Sacrifice

I learned a lesson from one of my clients, who is an investor. The first thing he asks a client is, "Let's go out for coffee." He arrives extremely early for the meeting. He notices who the person is, he notices what the person drives, what they order, and he notices their lifestyle cues. If he sees that the person drives a nice car and is concerned about how they look, he knows that the person may not have the sense of sacrifice required to personally invest in their business. You can tell the people that are going to make it in any business. If you don't have skin in the game and are not all in, you will not create a vibrant business.

You also don't want to create a jail cell made of gold. The trick is making the time you spend count. If you sacrifice sleep or time with family, the critical activity is to make the time count. Put away the phone and be completely present when you are with your family. The same is true when you are making moves in your business. Give each area of your life its proper attention. You may initially spend 12-14 hours engaging in the business, you will find that as the business develops, the 12 hours will reduce to 10 and later to 8 hours. The balance of time will return to your family and other activities that matter. Your family will not remember the amount of time you spent in the business of other activities. They will remember the impression, the engagement, the presence you communicated while you were completely present with them.

Case Study Method

For example, this text utilizes the barbershop business. As we introduce the sections of this book, we will repeatedly refer to the new business and the tool created for use in the barbershop. St-Ble offers bulk SMS, text from a local number, voice capabilities, and text-message based contact forms. The feature set connects as a social media scheduler as well.

Rather than provide tasks for practice, the case studies provide a thought exercise for readers to consider as they work to comprehend the content in the section. As you explore relationships and strategies as the primary presentations in the text, consider the possibilities provided by tools like St-Ble. As the motto suggests, Good business needs great communication for longevity and sustained growth. St-Ble is the tool that leverages your relationships and upholds your strategy for excellence in your business.

RELATIONSHIPS

Chapter 1: The Relationship Manifesto

Relationships result when you come to terms with the identity of your business. Your business identity is a careful crafting of the types of interactions you will have with the people who support your business. These interactions are actions; however, they are also evident in what you call those supporters. Often, the term customer is used for the people who buy from you. The term employee is used for those who work for and with you. I made a conscious choice early in my business development to emphasize the type of relationship I desired to have with both those who purchase and those who work with me. Those who purchase are called guests in my barbershop business. This emphasizes how I intend to interact with them. They are present for a limited amount of time and should be afforded the highest level of service and courtesy. Those who work with me are called partners. I emphasize the fact that these people work alongside me to grow, develop, and represent the business. These basic insistent features of the barbershop lexicon ensure that we navigate the waters of longevity together.

These relationships start with the parallels of your morals and principals. Who you are as a person will reflect in your brand or business. After all, your creations are an extension of your mindset. When you breathe life into a brand, the brand develops its own identity. Whether it be an LLC or a corporation, your brand will eventually stand on its own. That does not mean that the brand is not a reflection of you. The apple will never fall far from the tree. I developed my approach while growing up in a family where entrepreneurship and service were a way of life.

Growing Up

Growing up in Yonkers, New York, I watched my father masterfully run several grocery stores. I felt like I was watching a movie. The way my father worked a room was forever engrained in my head. He was not simply a salesman. He was a businessman. He intuitively sensed the needs of people and had a knack for connecting with them on a personal level. The results were no less impressive than the interactions. He seemed to approach work with people as an opportunity rather than an obligation. Service was a way of life, not a chore.

Those interactions served as a guiding light when I opened my first barbershop. I have always professed that I knew how to do things before I knew how to do them. Every day, I learned. Every day, my mental library grew. I was not aware of what was developing until years later. Live in the moment, right? But what if you do not know that you are actually in a moment?

My father always wanted something more for us. His motto was, "Do better for your kids than you had for your life." He had an immigrant mentality. You must outwork everyone because nothing is given. Just to make it to America was a struggle. He endured more in that process than any day on the job. Work was not about making money alone. It was about making a life for the next generation. That work ethic was just the beginning of my business training. My father started first grade at 12 years old. He would always tell me that I had a leg up because I started school at four years old.

I was not born here. My children are first-generation Americans. They are the accumulation of the hard work that my parents and I put into our own journeys. My children were born here healthy and happy. That is an additional leg up. I came to New York when I was seven years old. I remember being trained from an early age to be a hard worker. My father became more comfortable as I grew. I don't think he was training me to be anything in particular. He was providing resources so that I could be useful. He prepared me for a life of service. He wanted me to move intentionally rather than waiting for things to be handed to me. Earning was not the focus, but money can result when service is genuinely rendered. He instilled the notion that you can have what you want, but you will have to work for it.

Store, School, and Answers

When I was tasked with operating the register, I was barely 12 years old. I had no idea what I was doing. But do you think my father held my hand? I laugh because the answer is absolutely not. Those times taught me math in a way that school would never teach me.

Speaking of school, I dreaded the educational institution. So much emphasis was placed upon education that I could not enjoy it. I began to resent the focus. I remember lessons to this day because of the way I approached school. There were no such things as no-homework days. If I excelled, great. But if I made a mistake and received a bad grade, my father would make me memorize chapters. I developed a utilitarian relationship with school—I would do what I needed to and excel so that I could get school out of the way. My father would emphasize that I should always know that a problem can be solved. You only need the information, instructions, and search within yourself. He would always say that the answers are inside of you. He would lament that all the information was at my fingertips through computers, but I only used it to play games. He always directed me to look it up. He never told me the why. That was the missing piece that I now share with my kids. "You still need to do it, but this is why."

The practice of store management was a great teacher. My father would always caution to read people's intentions. "The more information you have, the better the information you can make." He would ask me about people and their mannerisms as they came into the store. I knew he was going to ask, so I would prepare myself. I became attentive to details; the little things so that I could address the large things. Those times taught me to read the room and the person walking into the store for purchase or possibly rob us. See, I learned how to read your thoughts, emotions, and mood based on how much weight you threw around with your walk. Who am I? Sometimes I look back and truly appreciate that upbringing. Without it, I believe I would not be successful today.

For example, I tell my partners, "Focus on the little things. Make sure your counter is clean. A clean counter says more than any sales pitch." It reminds me of my father's counsel.

"Someone may tell you that they are hungry but take a look at their sneakers. If they have new sneakers on but say they are hungry, they are lying. They are there to take advantage of you." It is a lesson in non-verbal communication. Guests are going to hear who you are through what you do and how you keep your environment as well as what you say. Language is a critical element of communication, but it is only one component. Nonverbals are important as well. Your guests are influenced by your actions, and they respond to the influence you create. When we talk about relationships, we are concerned with the influences that may be termed customer service, customer satisfaction, or relationship management. The key take away is to realize that you can use non-verbals to support guest behavior as well as their satisfaction. Rather than setting rules and enforcing them, you can create a healthy environment and influence compliance. The difference is more than semantic. It is behavioral.

For example, you may not want someone to be on the phone while you are cutting their hair. For relational reasons, you may not want to say directly, "Phones are prohibited in my chair." That is not the best customer service approach. You would do better to allow a person to answer the phone if it happens. Step away, still your scissors, or turn off your clippers. The client will look at you. They may say, "Oh no. Keep cutting."

Verbally, you respond with, "This is your hair cut. You drive the experience." Most people will end the call as soon as possible. They are going to put the phone away feeling uncomfortable on the phone. What they are feeling is, I need to put the phone away. What they are hearing is, I am in the driver's seat. And that's the message you want to communicate. This is a healthy environment rather than an environment of rules.

Approaching Business

When I applied those principles, as a young business owner, I didn't know if I was doing the right thing. All I knew was that it felt like I was doing the right thing. I remember clients traveling 1 hour and passing by countless barbershops to get a haircut from me of. The irony is that my father's clients would walk ten plus New York blocks, passing by a bodega on every corner, to only spend money at my father's store. The parallel is that both sets of clients preferred our business because of how we made them feel.

If you take pride in your business, it will show. If you treat everyone the way you would like to be treated, your business shall prosper. Take pride in developing an honest relationship with both customers and partners alike. The blessings will be endless. The success will be significant and provide stability via longevity. To this day, both businesses stand. My father sold to one of his partners that used to clean up the bodega. The barbershop is still in New Jersey, with many of the same customers from so many years ago. The only difference was the transfer of ownership between cousins; cousins who shared similar upbringings and a passion which made our dreams a reality. Those same relationships were a driving force for success.

Section Case Study

The importance of starting a relationship and maintaining it. Build relationships, not a clientele base. My father was keen on this point. Customers are people like you. It's not about how much money they would give you. Meet their needs. Once you meet their needs, they will take care of you. They are going to spend the money regardless. If you lead with their best interest, they will continue to spend with you. This breeds loyalty, which leads to sustained growth. Honesty, genuineness, and communication, which comes from caring about what you are doing and who you are doing it with. They won't seek anyone else because of the price loses importance, but because the value is overwhelming.

St-ble will not do the work for you, but it will facilitate the communication for you. You have 500 clients, and all your clients are texted at once. When you have a birthday entered, the tool will communicate the happy birthday each year without you needing to remember 500 client birthdays. No one tool is the reason for your success. You are vital to the mix. You must care about your clients. The tool can help you show that care.

Chapter 2: Customer Relationships: Guests

Severely undervalued, and hardly ever leveraged. We live in a time where social media, for the most part, makes the world revolve around us. That is a generalized statement, and by no means, am I committing everyone to the same analysis. The reality being, social media has transformed some professions into rockstars and blurred the lines of the art of the service. The mantra, "the customer is always right" is slowly disappearing. The customer-first mentality has de-evolved into a "you are lucky to be getting a haircut from me" type of attitude. Feel free to substitute haircut with any other service. I have noticed that professionals forget that we are here to serve. Our patron's needs are to be prioritized before our needs. To truly make an impact on longevity in the service industry, we must return to interactions that make the customer feel empowered, respected, and valued. Welcome to customer relations.

Customer By Another Name

I do not call my guest customers or clients. They are guests. I
want each person to feel comfortable when spending money with
me. In my barbershop business, I strive to create a home-like
atmosphere. The more I treat people like guests in my home, the
more loyalty they show, and the more comfortable they are. The
relationship with our business is different. It is not about
increasing traffic, hoping to get a percentage of the people
coming in and out. My intention is for guests to become
emotionally involved in the growth of the business. This business
treats you like family. You want to spend time with the people
you care about and who care about you. It just also happens to
be a business.

The most important thing for any for-profit business is the
customer. Their weight of importance is a line that has been
gradually blurred, especially in the service industry. We tend to
overshadow the things that we need to do with the expectance of
business. There is a certain level of professionalism that needs to
be met just to open the doors. Having a clean establishment,
having your licenses in order, and creating an environment are
only a few things that need to be done. Those things are not the
reason that customers should come into your establishment.
They create your minimum viable product. The bar that
professionals set is higher than the minimum. Your customers
will be patrons solely because of how they feel about your
establishment. How you make your customers think will last a

lifetime as well as usher in loyalty and a word of mouth marketing reaction unparalleled by any other.

Observation: What your guests spend will be emotionally tied to how they felt when they made the purchase. How they felt in your establishment will live forever in their memory. It is our duty, in the service industry, to hyper-focus on this notion. Assuming that your goal is a prosperous business, you must be intentional about creating and managing emotions. I have seen many climb to a level of influence only to fall from grace. The common denominator among fallen businesses is not putting the customer first. It is beyond titles like sir and madam. We always call people with their first name, but also any title that is appropriate. Mr. and Miss make sense sometimes. Doctor is appropriate for some. In my barbershop, we take notes of what clients like to be called as well. The respect of learning someone's name, nickname, or their definition of self-related to their profession is critical in putting the person first.

Karma

The successful behaviors that have benefited the businesses I have had the pleasure of growing are personalized attention, expressed commitment, and mining for details. When a customer walks into the store, everything stops. Everyone that is not a customer has the responsibility of a warm and inviting greeting.

No exceptions. This principle was developed when I was still young in business working in retail.

I remember when a customer came in to return an item she purchased. The store manager and I found each other on different sides of the customer; engrossed in an argument. I was of the mindset that she was just trying to get over on the store. In my mind, that return was going to put us into the red for the day, and I was not trying to hear it. The store manager was of the mindset of not losing a customer.

I met her with an attitude. The manager greeted her with an offer of water or coffee. She spoke her piece about what she wanted to return. I heard inconsistencies while the manager saw a problem with our product. I was standing because she was past the return window. In contrast, the manager was apologetic that our product didn't live up to what was advertised. The customer wanted her money back. I wanted her out of the store because of the negative impact I assumed she was having on other customers. That day, I learned a lesson that will forever stay with me. The manager not only refunded her, even though it was clear she was trying to get over on us but offered a complimentary product to apologize for not meeting her expectations. She declined and took the refund.

Obviously, I was confused as to why we would take such a hit. Then, karma instantly showed up. The manager did the right thing, which was noticed by a customer standing quietly in observance. That second customer went on to have the most significant order of the month. That customer respected how the return situation was handled. She pledged support to any product that a company stands that firmly behind. That attitude created a client that now, some ten years later, is still showing loyalty.

If I had had my way, I would have irrevocably done damage. Not only to the customer making the return but to the one observing. To this day, I think about how many other customers were gained because of how that return was handled. That is a commitment that every business should have. How you make your customers feel will keep the door to success wide open.

The initial contact of a customer is so important and severely underused. In the barbering industry, more often than not, we have the privilege of knowing who will be walking through our doors. Imagine if you are a new or repeating customer, being greeted by your name as you walk in. How would that make you feel?

Granted, this is for an appointment-only model where you can collect identifying information. If it is not in that wheelhouse, a simple, what is your name will go a long way. Asking them for a name and how their day is going before you ask, "how can I help you" is a technique that resonates. Your customers will feel like you are not only after their money but are committed to them. Perception is king. We know the customer is there to spend money, that is a given, or they wouldn't have walked through the door. Our manner of approach either affirm that decision or drive them away. Spending two seconds to acknowledge your customers before closing the sale will make the sale running a lot smoother.

Without the sale hanging over your head, you can start to develop a relationship. That relationship will bring you success. That relationship will create a comfort level among your customers that will influence their loyalty. That relationship is instrumental in the growth of your business.

You alone need to understand that you may not connect with your customers. Your goal to accomplish is respect. They may not invite you into their lives, but will only go to you for the service that you provide. That is the definition of loyalty. That is the reason mutual respect is so important. If a customer feels like you are trying to sell them, they will usually back off. On the other hand, if a customer feels like you genuinely care about them, the connection will be made.

Personalization

Every single second that the customer is in your establishment should be individually leveraged to building a relationship. From the greeting to the time they are in the store to the time they are exiting. Especially when leaving your business. At this time, appreciation is vital. Honest appreciation will be noticed. Forced appreciation will leave your customers with a bad taste in their mouths. Think about it; when you say thank you, that is the last impression they will have of you for this interaction.

While the customer is getting serviced, I am on a recon mission. I am asking questions about their plans for the rest of the day, week, or month. I am asking about anything exciting in their lives or anything they may be looking forward to. That information should be put in your customer's notes. When you deal with a large group of people, some of those details may escape your thoughts. Notes help you remember those details. Notes are important. When saying thank you follow it by a personalized statement. For example, "thank you for visiting. I appreciate the business and hope you get that promotion you've been working on." When the guest returns, you have already read the notes and prepared for the interaction. Your comments that connect with their last meeting will engage them instantly. "How was your daughter's recital?" Or, "How is that promotion going?" The personalization goes a long way toward creating loyalty and continuing an engaging dialogue.

Personalization says that the guest is important and valued. These details will have a lasting and favorable impression. This commitment should be operationalized every time you see a customer, no exceptions. For that, every time you see a customer, you have the opportunity to keep their business. Customers are not yours and will never be. Every encounter should be an additional reason why they continue to give you their interests, time, and money. The customer is always right. Without the customer, there is no business. Treat them like guests. Take our lead and call them that. Guests are your bread and butter. Act accordingly.

Chapter 3: Employee Relationships: Partners

It is no secret; ownership breeds pride. That is the principle of the American dream. As many flaws as that statement holds, the underlying idea is accurate. When you own a business, you tend to care more about its success. When you are an employee, the clocking in and out mentality can hinder growth. Throughout my career, I have always looked for a solution to this often-overlooked problem. Barbershops are a revolving door for clientele and professionals alike. You keep the client loyal by having a strong customer relations program. On the other hand, you keep professionals dependable by implementing a revenue-sharing initiative.

Yet, in the interest of full disclosure, understand that revenue sharing will not be enough. You must cultivate an environment anchored in growth, respect, and one that will challenge the professional. The goal is to involve everyone so that they are inspired to give 100 percent effort all the time. Revenue sharing is how you can take your business to the dream destination amongst professionals. Logistics and details must be worked out to reflect on the capabilities of your business. A pay re-structure may be appropriate. All of these methods should be discussed thoroughly with your attorney and accountant. For the relevance of this chapter, let's assume your business is capable of implementing a profit-sharing initiative. Let's dive into the reason why that thought process will be beneficial. The thought process creates an opportunity to view employees in a different light. Through the sharing of financial benefit, they become more partners than employees. In my businesses, my employees are always considered to be partners.

Creating Culture

Creating the culture is the work of your business. The place where you do business is a building. The culture is what makes the building come alive. You have plenty of places where an individual can work, but there are fewer places where one can grow. Growth is the reason you go to work. That may seem to be an overstatement for some. You do what you need to do to make the money, and you go home. But, when there is a culture that you buy into, your thoughts throughout the day are about improving, contributing, and innovating the business. Culture of progress inspires you to improve your workflow and your interaction success with guests. Culture of teamwork motivates you to contribute in multiple ways to the daily functioning of the team. Culture of efficiency compels you to seek and implement cutting edge technology and techniques.

Hiring is a major consideration influencing culture. Done well, it is focused on the morals, principals, and the culture beyond just talent and skill. The person must mesh with the culture of the business. Their character must fit. We bring candidates into the shop with the intention to show them the experience of working with our team. We notice how they interact, how they respond, and how they engage with amenities in the space. They are invited to engage with the guests and expand the interview through interactions with them. One rule of thumb we use is that if a person never picks up the broom during an interview, they are not hired. The barbershop offers multiple opportunities for an "all in this together" culture. We seek that principal displayed actively in the mentality and actions of candidates.

Training and Development

From good to exceptional is our intention. "Build the professional, and the professional will grow the business." As an owner, those sayings should be on permanent repeat in your mind. Every decision should stem from those principles. No need to over complicate it or find another solution. It is simple, cultivate a winning environment through empowerment. Place the professionals you work with in a position to win. Think of the professional as working with you instead of working for you.

A common boardroom story suggests that an inexperienced Human Resources professional asks the owner, "What if we train them and they leave?" To which the wise CEO responds, "What if we don't train them and they stay?" The sentiment expressed by the wise CEO speaks to an additional investment beyond profit sharing; calculated in the bottom line in the same way. These are investments in your partners and cultivation of a partner culture.

I am not possessive in MY business. The use of the word "my" is possessive. Over time, that has proven to create resentment. I mean, how many times have you heard I built that company for them, or I opened up that store. When the word "my" is used, and the compensation doesn't match, it has led to a bad taste in someone's mouth. The concept should be substituted by "ours." This is our shop vs. this is my shop. Saying "our" places your business in a different light. Sometimes difficult decisions need to be made, and if the company is separate from the owner, those decisions can be easier to make.

Let's face it; no one wants to do all the work just for someone else to benefit from it. Understanding that the owner will take more risks for the business, no professional wants to feel like it was accomplished on their backs. That is the reality, but there is a solution. Share the decision making. Share the financial benefits. Affirm an US and OURS culture.

I challenge each of my partners to improve their skill in the technical aspects of their job. I also ask them to enhance their conversational skills. I expect my partners to engage at a greater level than the employees of our competitors. I have asked them to know the news and understand their views on aspects expected at our shop. Our clientele represents a specific demographic. The conversation that they find engaging is based on current events, financial considerations, and corporate newsmakers.

Our guests are doing more than living paycheck to paycheck. They are looking to maintain wealth, make smarter investments, and engage in work-life balance. They expect professionals around them to engage with respect, competence, and intelligence. At the same time, there is no requirement to know everything. Listening and learning can be just as engaging as speaking. "I don't know," is golden in this business. We can't relate to every client who has billionaire status on the money, but we can show genuine interest in the person, their challenges, hopes, and daily pressures. One strategy is to ask questions rather than thinking that you must provide all the answers. My partners enhance the guest's experience when they are conversant in their interests. I also suggest that partners become experts in interviewing. The benefit is two-fold. Many of our guests enjoy sharing information. Partners gain insights that they would pay for elsewhere. Guests like to be interviewed. Most are engaged when you ask them questions about the topic they engage with during their daily lives. The trust the guest gives as they allow you to cut their hair is multiplied in return as they find opportunity to share their expertise.

Communication

Communication is key. Have a conversation about the business's financial needs. In the spirit of shared governance, share as much of this with your partners as is practical. This creates a level of buy-in that can be rare in the corporate world. Set a clear and precise goal. A goal that involves everyone is one that supports full awareness. It is a goal that everyone can participate in achieving. When partners know the financial benefit of switching off lights or guest engagement, for example, they are more likely to own these behaviors as acts of pride and work ethic.

The emphasis is on teamwork. Ensure that the purpose satisfies the needs and wants of the business. Once that goal is achieved, divide the profits accordingly among the team. With professionals and owners alike. Be sure to pay on schedule, whether it be monthly, quarterly, or yearly. The message should be loud and clear. The feeling and actualization that we are in our business together will resonate with everyone involved.

That culture will also resonate with the customers. There is no better feeling than going to a store and observing employees that love their job. The experience of these guests is elevated. The time spent at that business will have an impact on the customer long after they leave. Customer relations and partner relations go hand in hand. Ying and Yang, one compliments the other.

Success is about harmony. Harmony between the guest and partner. The responsibility to create this harmony falls on the owner. It is their duty to ensure that both parties are happy with the process as well as the outcome. This is the power of a partner culture energized by profit sharing.

DEVELOPING A BUSINESS

Chapter 4: The Strategies

Theories compliment practice. That is a commonly accepted academic fact. In business situations, strategies support relationships. Strategies help you discover the voice of your business that speaks to your guests. The messages they receive create an experience. When strategies are appropriate to the business, consistent in application, and supportive of positive guest experiences, they make your business into an efficient revenue-generating machine.

Get into the habit of conducting research. Once you have the information, everything is easier. You can look up your desired name. You can secure your Instagram and other social media properties. What happens is, if you don't know what is going on in your market, you will behind the 8-ball all the time. You are going to be reactive. You don't want to be reactive. You want to lead. Those who lead will set the pace, price, and purpose within the industry. Market research conditions you to the value of information and being ahead of the curve.

No matter what you are doing, you must start with a genuine interest. After that, your path is set by curiosity. The fear and trepidation lessen as you recognize that your only requirement is to get the information within the area you desire to sell. If you are interested, you will do market research without any person telling you to do so. For example, you likely want to start a business because you have already noticed something missing in the market. You notice the needs of customers, the deficits within the market, and the competition or lack thereof. Nothing keeps you moving and motivated more than curiosity.

That is an Option A scenario. Option B also exists. If you don't have the interest, but you know that the market is viable, find someone with the interest that doesn't have the capacity. Continue to develop yourself in the areas that fit your market and the problem you are solving. As opposed to interest, motivate yourself through a desire to learn and develop as a professional. Treat it like you are a scholar, and you are inspired to grow the business through research.

Foundations of Research

To understand any strategy, you first have to know the source. Where is the strategy coming from, and has it proven to be effective? Taking a closer look. How many times has it worked? Are you willing to follow the instructions? This is critical. I have learned that commitment is as important as the execution. Countless times, I have seen the creative cook blame the recipe when her augmentations fail in taste and presentation. Condemning the method always comes down to a question of accountability. Be responsible for your actions. Before you take the leap of faith, make sure you will be landing on firm ground. Not coincidently, that firm ground happens to be the strategies in the following chapters. These are time tested and proven to be effective across multiple industries in different markets. These strategies, if followed precisely, will save you time, money, and energy. Follow the recipe with fidelity and reap the results suggested.

Before we get into those strategies, allow me to prepare you for my interpretation of knowledge sharing. Growing up in my environment, I was never given step by step instructions. Ever. Assigning blame and finger pointing aside, the reason was Antonio Sosa. A devoted husband and father, an accomplished entrepreneur, and proud Latino. My father has a doctorate in biochemistry from the Soviet Union. The methodology of my upbringing was a direct relationship to the foundation of his education. He would point me in the best direction to access the information needed to achieve whatever it was that he wanted me to learn. Instead of giving me answers, or by his definition, the easy way out, he would make me work for it. And when I showed interest in learning, he was even vaguer. As you can imagine, this approach is immensely frustrating for an adolescent.

I was always tasked to conduct research. My frustration built as I could never get a definitive answer. I remember the thoughts that ran through my head when I asked a question. At the moment, those thoughts were never verbalized due to fear. If you are not aware, that is an average Hispanic household. Frustrating in my memories, but later conflicted with gratefulness at present moments of appreciation.

My father's favorite saying was, "did you read the directions?" Knowing that most of the things that I wanted to learn seldom come with instructions. How to throw a baseball, how to ride a bike, or even how to understand the Fibonacci sequence. He assumed I was at a higher level of understanding, which I had to fulfill to gain his respect. My father was adamant about using technology for research and would often direct me to my computer to find answers. He would get frustrated when I would use technology for entertainment. To this day, when I do use technology for leisure, I usually am alone. That upbringing has developed into a "question everything" type of philosophy for my adult life. I am exploring, investigating, questioning product of my environment due to the conditioning to research anything and everything.

Realism and Market Research

Many people go into a business with the idea that they will be unique, overthrow their competition, and establish a chokehold on market share. There is nothing new under the sun, as the adage goes. Your business would need to be extremely cutting edge to be new. We often just add a few things. We take away things. What we end up with is something different, but not necessarily unique.

In a coffee shop example, you are not going to beat out a larger company that has more buying power. You are going to pay more for coffee and other vital materials because you do not have the customer base or sales to buy supplies at a low price like the larger company.

Most of my barber students want to make $100,000 per year as a barber. I inform them that they are not going to achieve that goal. They are convinced that they can. My point is not to simply rain on their dreams. I am making a point about how to bolster their dreams with research.

I ask them how much their target income calculates to per week. They don't know. They state that they will just add it up at the end of the year. That is not business. I ask them, how many haircuts their target income translates into per week. The point is that they need to approach business beyond the bravado and desires for success. Their business success hinges upon their ability to create intentional goals by breaking big dreams into tangible actions.

Many of my students want to cut celebrities. They think their skill will set them apart and have them cutting the top stars in the movies. I tell them that it is not going to happen. They ask why I am being so negative. I explain that Jay-Z's barber has been cutting his hair for 19 years. His name is Johnny. He lives in New Jersey. The only way Jay-Z is going to get a new barber is if Johnny recommends someone personally. The celebrities that you see already have stylists, personal style, and comfort with their look. They are not looking to hire new people and train them according to their sensitivities, quirks, and proclivities. Your best option as a new barber is to find new artists and connect with them. Deliver a style portfolio and options. Create a relationship that you can build upon for the future.

Market Research is your first step. You want to know the market competition and market share targets. Next, look beyond the glamorous components to the mundane tasks. Will your vision work financially and practically? Identify the margins that would be required. You detail the amount of energy required to achieve your vision. Determine whether you are willing to consistently put that level of energy into the business. Determine whether you want a static location, to travel, or some combination. Consider the time you want with family versus the time you are willing to sacrifice if necessary. Finally, consider whether you are willing to commit. The decisions you make now will be the foundations of your business. They will mean the difference between failure and success.

Attention to Detail

I have performed the trial and error so that you do not have to. Agonizing over the details, I developed a unique skill set which you are about to benefit from. I have done the leg work. I have figured out how to launch a business from all angles. Taking into account names, trademark, social media presence, and growth mindsets. The next chapters pay homage to my father by showing you the way. Instead of a simple step by step tutorial that leaves out the drama and heart, I focus on why things should get done—your motivation, challenges, and ways to overcome setbacks. Sure, I go into detail for options as to where and or how to get those things done. But I also leave room for you to do your own research and navigate the diverse waters of your business. The focus is on the end destination; even while you put in the effort required. This is the blueprint. You must do the traveling on your own.

Section Case Study

Strategy and tools are important to comprehend. Once you know what you need to do, your task is to identify how to execute the strategy with the least amount of investment and resistance. The strategy implementation is dependent upon the tools available to you. When a great tool and a great strategy come together, excellence results. The lines between mediocre strategy and better strategy are blurry in the minds of some. You will want to clarify the lines. You would never park your Lamborghini of a strategy on the muddy floored ground of an inferior tool.

When people ask what makes St-Ble different, my answer is that it is proven. It is what my barbershop uses. I was not thinking about expanding it for other businesses until a client asked about our system. He was impressed by the ease and responsiveness of the tool, thinking that it was a live team of receptionists and customer engagement personnel. "No. It's just one integrated tool.

We are using St-Ble with amazing results. I have an average of 1800 guests through my chair every 45 days. I see the value of the tool with every engagement and satisfied customer. From the messages an hour before the appointment to the messages to reschedule. No call-no shows were reduced. Rescheduling is more efficient. The people that make their appointments are always satisfied with the details we were taking care of. Automated messages, voice lines, and social media features integrated into one system will be available to other shops for a low monthly fee.

Chapter 5: The Name Strategy

The success of your business depends on how much you can put your personal feelings aside. No matter how much you want something, you must approach it in a business mindset. No area is more important than the name of the company. Separate yourself from the business and create an identity that connects with your customers. No matter how much you put into the business, the business is not you. It is created to appeal to your customers.

Asking the Right Questions

Being an educator, the most frequent question I get asked is, "How do I start?" Which is usually the first probe in a long line of questions. How do I start is commonly followed by, "Do you think it will make me money?" Humbled, I appreciate getting asked this question because it shows that whoever is asking values my opinion. Even though I am grateful, I feel obligated to break down what is wrong with this line of questioning.

For starters, no one's judgment during the inception of your idea or business should influence the trajectory of your path. I believe we over complicate things because we get ahead of ourselves. It is more than understandable; we get excited. That is natural yet expected, so let's pump the breaks and take a deep breath.

No matter how much people sugarcoat the experience, you get into business to make money. People will tell you that you must love what you do. But this is not the primary concern. Consider that if someone offers you a business that will provide six figures of income in an area that you do not enjoy, the business is not a poor business. You could still benefit from the business even if you do not enjoy it. In fact, you can hire someone to manage the business who likes it and take a 50% take of the revenue. You still win.

You are looking for a return on your investment when you start a business. This is primary. You want it to be sustainable after a defined amount of time. Prefacing your initial question, "Will this make me money?" you should do your due diligence and vet your idea before taking outside influences. If it is your idea, then it is YOUR idea. If you are looking to partner with someone or a group, include them in the inception and the discovery.

For the sake of argument, let's assume you wholeheartedly believe that you have a great idea. Belief is the fuel for a long journey ahead. That road is far from straight and full of twists and turns. Your ability to secure your fundamentals, notice the details, and respond to the unexpected will determine your experience through the journey.

The Name

First and foremost, what will you name it? I cannot stress enough
how important this step is. The doubt that manifests the
question, "Is this the right name? " will never go away. There will
always be that voice in your head playing the devil's advocate.
For some, that voice is louder than others. I get it. The name will
be the hardest thing to change once you decide. So, here is what
helped me ease my mind and guide me to fully committing.

The clarity of your name is important. The two areas you must
be concerned with are trademarks and social media. This is the
foundation of your brand. You must tell the story with the brand
and protect that messaging with the trademark and social media
registration process. You want people to follow your story no
matter where they are introduced to it.

I start by searching the United States Patent and Trademark
Office (www.uspto.gov) for any legally documented uses of the
name I would like to use. This website has a ton of information
that will help your business. Time should be spent on it to
familiarize yourself with how things work in the trademark
world.

Once you take a look around, make your way to the Trademark
Electronic Search System or commonly abbreviated as
"TESS." (http://www.tmsearch.uspto.gov) Since this is the very
beginning, start with a "basic word mark" search. On that

window, make sure the option for "plural and singular" is checked as well as "live and dead." Type in your name and then click on "submit query." When your search comes back, you will be able to see all the instances the name you selected has been used. If "live" trademark results come back, you'll need to come up with another name. If "dead" or a blank search comes back, then you have a green light to continue to the next step.

Social Media and the Internet

I usually use GoDaddy as my domain registrar, but there's a ton of them out there. Make sure that they are credible before you do any business. Search for your name. Ideally, you should be looking for a (.)com. This is because com is a top-level domain (TLD), categorizing it as a must own. Now for some businesses, a different domain ending is required or should be used. For example, an online academy named "lxve" would be more appealing if the domain is lxve.academy rather than lxveacademy.com. In this instance, I would purchase both domains, build on the com, and have the academy point to the latter. The purpose is for search engine optimization (SEO) purposes. Search engines will index you higher if your domain ends in com. That is not my call, just the rules that are set by companies like Google, Bing, and Yahoo.

The next step is to do a social media search to see if anyone else is using your future company's name. Doing things in this order will save you a lot of headaches and back and forth between steps. Although social media will be your anchor in digital advertising, if your name is not available, it will not mean that you have to come up with another name. Sometimes your name may not be possible to claim. No worries, a direct message to the user could reveal if he or she is willing to sell. Let's say they are not enthusiastic about giving up your desired username. Consider adding just about anything to your username to make it available. For example, Paper is more than likely not available on any social media platforms, but GetPaper or Paper-less will probably be available. For this walkthrough, let's say the desired username is available. And when I say available, I mean across as many channels as you can access. The same name because continuity is essential. Even if you will not be using a particular platform, sign up regardless. Securing those channels will always be a good idea.

Once you have collected this information, it is time to act. Begin by purchasing your domain name. That purchase will open up the ability to create a professional email with that name, i.e., info@lxveacademy.com. The best part is that you have options. Do your homework in email hosting and select the one that best suits your needs. For me, I chose privacy and went with hey.com as opposed to companies that store your data on their servers.

With your new email, register your brand for every social media platform possible. I usually start with Twitter, Instagram,

Facebook, and then work my way to others like Tik-Tok and Snapchat.

Once all this is done, I strongly recommend reaching out to a trademark lawyer and talking about legally owning the name you have created. Depending on the nature of your business, this step may be crucial to your success and not leave the door open for a big problem down the line. Like I said, depending on your business, you might not need to trademark your name. This step is relevant to your situation.

The bottom line is that your name is essential. Following these steps means that you can invest in your brand without the fear of wasting money. Completing these steps signify that you are without a doubt in control of your name. Stepping on firm ground, you can begin to build on the layers of success.

Chapter 6: The Team Strategy

A village is required to serve a business as well as to raise a child. Too many fail to recognize the value of a strong team of professionals. The loss of time, energy, and other resources from getting new team members up to speed takes a toll on the final presentation of your product. If you do not pay the appropriate costs upfront, you will pay more later on. You cannot move forward while you are constantly starting over.

In business, it can be said that the front office is the megaphone. The back office is the voice. In the front office, your partners are going to interact with the clients. The back office created the uniforms, the ambiance, the policies and procedures that govern the interactions. The development of this team is critical to your success. They have the monumental task of governing the actions of your partners.

This chapter is designer heavy because of the process of business development. It details the approach for ensuring that the back office professionals set the look and feel of your brand. They are the story weavers of your brand. Your designer is critical to the development of your business. When other team members are added, they will refer back to the designer for guidance.

Types of Teams

Sure, you can find someone who can create an excellent logo or a fantastic profile picture. I can also see how the cheapest route, especially at this stage, can seem like the best option. It is understandable but let me explain why you should be thinking in terms of team and longevity.

When you think team, think of all types of collateral you will be creating. Would you need, in addition to a logo, videos, animations, and a website, to say the least? The answer is probably yes. I want you to think about continuity for your brand. Continuity is one of the pillars for long term success. Think of your collateral as a voice. Would you want to change your voice after you have already established your collateral? Logically the answer is no, but let's analyze why brand voices are often changed.

Collateral profiles get changed simply because of putting the cart before the horse. The development of a brand is consistently overshadowed by the need for validation. Designers get changed when the two parties have a disagreement in price and or opinions of direction. That inconsistency can be pinpointed to using different graphic designers, web developers, and animators from the initial design. Every creative has his or her own style of creating. Every time projects are completed by a different person, the voice will change. At this stage in development, it may not seem like a big deal. In my experience, it is always best to prevent a problem rather than creating one. Continuity leads to brand dependability. Brand dependability creates long term success.

Interviewing Skills

Interview your freelancers, partners, and other team members on how long they are interested in doing what they are working on. Their longevity is important to your sustainability. I have a long-term designer. If I tell him about a project I am working on, I must only tell him the media. He knows the color pallet, styles, and shapes that I am comfortable with. I do not need to spend extra time in interviews describing my tastes and preference.

What I suggest, select a team. Interview various designers. Get a sense of their creativity. Understand how they process work, what is the turnaround time, and the quality of delivered collateral. Then explain to your potential designer what your goals are and how you plan on involving them for the whole life of the brand. This will create a consistency that will benefit you by having some type of preference, as well as a probable discounted price point.

Most designers are freelancers and will more than likely work with you when they know you are trying to guarantee them to work for a prolonged period. Designers tend to be more committed when they are aware of directing all the media associated with a brand. This gives them a sense of ownership. That sense of ownership will mean that the designer will take even more pride in their work than they already do. This scenario has been proven to give the fruit of the best possible results.

I suggest starting with an established designer because they have resources. They have animators and developers that they consistently work with. They have a tribe of creatives that they respect. All you have to do is ask for admission. Professionally and politely. This will be crucial in helping to form your team. Creating one point of contact rather than many will be a lot easier to manage.

Starting out, you may pay your designer by project, but as you continue to grow, start thinking of having him or her on a retainer type of agreement. Again, not thinking about right now instead of anticipating your needs before they arrive. Efficiency is as a result of proper preparation.

Core Principles

Find out the core principles and values of the people you are looking to work with. An interview that is formal will only yield so much. Informal talk is not the way to engage either. You want to engage the person in the practice of who they are. The best way to do that is to invite them to a function. In my barbershop, we have them hang with us for the day. As a team, we pay attention to who they are, how they act, and how they respond to opportunities for pitching in. I need people who have that all-for-one mentality.

You can find out a lot about people by reviewing their social media. This is a useful business tool today. In an interview, most candidates are prepped for the questions that the typical employer asks. When I look at your social media, that will tell me more informally who you are. The pages often can be mined for your favorites, your interests, your temperament, and more related to your social profile. A few minutes on your timeline and a solid comparison can be made between the culture we desire and your mindset. For designers and the back-office team, it is important to have people who evidence creativity, diversity, and skill even in their social profiles.

Finally, working with potential team members, you may find more about a potential long-term member after the initial work is done. The best people will under promise and over deliver. They will demonstrate an ethic of outworking the competition in their chosen field. These are those you will want to engage in retainer type arrangements. Retaining allows you to leverage the expertise and professionalism of the team member to visualize new directions for your business. You know you can count on them, which allows you to step into opportunities beyond your expertise and capability.

Chapter 7: The Logo Strategy

You have named your brand, hopefully, trademarked, bought a domain, and registered for every single social media platform available. You have also come up with a name and took the necessary precautions to protect your investment. Naturally, your next inclination would be to start creating collateral such as logos, banners, profile pictures, headers, and so on. You have found a designer and outlined the opportunity for a team, and they have helped you put together a tribe that can accomplish all of your graphic needs. So, what is next?

The Logo Imperative

Let's talk about logo design, or better known as the blueprint for your brand moving forward. The logo is essential because it will influence your brand every step of the way. From color schemes to shapes, your logo is the initial message delivered to your target audience. Think of a logo in terms of a first impression. You want a consistent presentation to meet each person no matter how they engage with your brand. Your goal is to begin to associate some version of positive regard central to the client with your brand. You want to be seen as a vital solution to the challenges that they are facing.

Since we are talking about a logo, I will assume that you have a designer in place. One that you have thoroughly vetted and are confident can deliver at the quality that is on-brand. On brand means that the presentations of your brand are consistent. No confusion exists when someone views your environment, digital media, or print media. It means that you are putting out linkages, often visually but also aurally in some cases, to your audience. If your brand is luxury, your logo should reflect that message. The same goes for urban, contemporary, and every other category. Think it through before you act.

Understand that the logo dictates your presence, style, and story across all the media it is printed on. The shapes, colors, and mood will extend from the logo. Everything you do after this in business must be consistent with the design suggested by your logo.

For example, the Pepsi Co, logo was updated a few years ago by a company that was simply interested in updating the logo. They sent over the specifications for the revised logo they spent over a year refining. Pepsi Co was initially cold to the idea of working with the company on the logo refresh but warmed gradually as the power and appeal of the revision set in. I believe the final purchase price to the design company was over $20 million for their services. Even for an iconic brand, they had created a compelling and irrefutable update capturing the direction of the company. Though they were outsiders, they seemed to know Pepsi better than they knew themselves. This is the level of insight you are hoping for when developing your logo. It should immediately speak to a feeling you want your customers to have.

Working with a Designer

There is a finesse that should be applied when doing business with a designer. For them to deliver optimal results, a specific approach is warranted. I should know because I am a designer myself. Throughout the years, I have analyzed my best works, as well as the ones that I am not as proud of. There is a consistent denominator. Time is money, and the wrong approach will be costly. Let's talk about how to navigate those waters.

Tasks you should do exist, and definitely, there are somethings that you should not do. Let us begin with the do-not to keep you from damaging your brand before you even launch any design elements. To keep this relationship in the best of standings, these are three cardinal rules that should be followed and never bent or broken.

1. Never tell a designer what program or tools to use. A talented and experienced designer will use whatever tool they deem fit. Let the designer chose the right tool to deliver on the quality you are looking for.

2. Do not approach a designer without a clear and precise direction. A designer is there to provide graphics and bring to life the message of your brand. Their job is not to create the company guidelines for you.

3. Finally, never allow your designer to chase you for payment. Once the job is completed, pay immediately. If you asked for a ton of revisions, tip well.

What you should not do is accounted for, let's discuss the proper way to conduct business with a designer.

1. Trust is the most impactful thing you give. I cannot emphasize enough the power of selecting the right team for the needs of your brand. Understanding where the application is vital in determining some of the necessary details in creating graphics. Such as dimensions, color profiles, sizing, and resolution. Saying this will be used, for example, as my brand's logo will be very much appreciated. With communication, your designer will know what format will be needed.

2. Ensure that you will receive multiple formats in your delivery. A great designer will deliver your logo in jpg, png ai, and icon formats. That means your logo can be applied to any and every medium imaginable.

3. Be aware of follow up questions when requesting graphics. I suggest being prepared so that you are ready to respond immediately. Sometimes you may describe

what you are looking for without the need for a follow-up list of questions. Usually, that is not the case. I recommend a phone call to prevent an endless chain of emails or texts, trying to explain those very details.

4. Here is a little secret about designing. It works off of inspiration. Once the inspiration hits, you want to make sure you have given every detail possible for creating the best logo for your brand. Do everything in your power to allow your designer to strike once the iron is hot.

Mindset and Preparation

Before you decide your brand needs a logo, have the following questions answered. What type of company, meaning what is the target audience? What color scheme fits that target audience the best, and would you like to incorporate a personal touch of your favorite color.

For example, the color purple signifies royalty. Do you have a brief description of your brand? You are not required to write anything long. A paragraph describing the brand's principal attributes, the feelings or images you want to inspire, and the emotions you want to elicit would be enough. Additional considerations depend upon the luxury level of your brand and business. Would you like a character, or do you prefer a script type of logo? The higher-end your brand, the less is more principle that should be applied. Think Tom Ford, Hermes, and

Goyard. The more your logo screams for attention, the less substance a brand usually has.

In my experience, your logo should state that your brand is serious and committed to providing an excellent service or product. If a logo is too loud, it symbolizes a weakness in that service or product that needs to be overshadowed. The busier the logo, the more it appears that you are trying to convince your audience. Your mindset should be to complement your brand with the logo and other design elements. This means that your logo is like a comfy chair that your brand settles into after a long day of advertising. When your customers see the logo, they should see comfort, compatibility, and function immediately. Even though you will be selling, any hint of trying too hard will cast a negative impression on your potential buyers.

When you experience a logo that is professionally designed, it resonates. It represents the brand and is an immediate choice over logos of lesser quality. Confidence is subconsciously ascribed to logos of high quality. It is similar to a business services employee candidate who attends an interview in sneakers and a t-shirt. She will not look the part and may be judged to be inferior to other candidates. Taking a look at successful companies throughout history, I have noticed that their logos, at times, cannot stand up as impressive visuals as the body of work the brand is known for. In hindsight, the logo was not the reason for its success. It is regarded as a flag for the principles and commitment of the brand. This suggests a potentially contradictory approach to logo design. Under promise with the logo and over-deliver in the details. This is not to say that you can phone in the logo design. It does say that a great logo without great customer service is worthless. The compatibility, that complementary relationship between brand and logo is visual and expressed through service. Consider this the most vital determining factor in elevating your business from good to exceptional.

Chapter 8: The Website Strategy

You have your name, you have your team, and you have your logo. Congrats. It is now time to talk about your virtual real estate. Some companies will not need a website. Some just want a website. Many miss the strategy behind a website. Let me start by saying that there are a ton of web developers and every more drag and drop imposters in the marketplace. Navigating those waters can be troublesome and end up costing time and resources. Luckily, you have read the team strategies chapter and have developed a great relationship with your designer. You may not have thought about a web developer before, but now is the time.

We must begin with the reasons why. Primarily, the website is used as a tool to help you sell. You must ask questions about how easy you make the website to sell. If there is information, do you push that information through with the connection to the sales activity. If they only want information upon a visit, you must provide the information that supports their decision to buy.

Sales are your goal. From there, you have decisions about design. People want actualized, modern, clean. They want it to load fast. Many people focus on everything other than sales and function. The website is a representation of you in the marketplace. Some make it what they want to see, and they forget about their target audience. Anything not targeted to your audience is a waste of money. You must understand your core market and your target audience. Great companies do not stray from their core product. Coca-Cola does not mix their message by selling t-shirts on their site.

Whether your website is for the presence or as a crucial part of your business, it is a must-have. It must be on brand. Especially with e-commerce, you want to enhance the experience for the buyer. If the experience is not up to par, a buyer will look for alternatives. If the experience is positive, the buyer is more likely to return as a customer and recommend others to you.

Presenting the Why

When you go to a site selling something you need. They focus on the why of your buying experience. The better companies connect with your why. They know this because you are their target audience. They have spent some time in market research, but beyond their research, they have developed an approach for speaking with their target audience.

The first answer for you is connecting with their why. Next is explaining why they should purchase from you rather than someone else. For my barbershop business, we answer the first why by making the experience targeted to those who want to book an appointment. This can be completed in three clicks. The ease creates a positive experience. It supports repeat usage. It also has the indirect benefit of reducing stress on our phone lines. I don't have to pay a receptionist to receive calls and book appointments all day. The benefits are exponential as the digital processes are integrated and easy for the customer.

The benefits boil down to process function and experience. My receptionist spends less time booking appointments and more time receiving our guests. She makes them feel comfortable and engages genuinely with them. She spends less time answering the phones and more time enhancing the experience of live guests.

Finding a Developer

Ask your designer who they recommend. I can guarantee that they have developed their own relationship with a web developer and have worked together countless times. They are typically going to recommend someone that they have a relationship and some rapport with. Even if they don't have one in mind, they may have knowledge of where to find a suitable web developer. Your website will stand above others because of this synergy among your team.

In some instances, your graphic designer is also a talented web developer. The fact that you built a relationship means that if they are in over their heads, they will be honest and not over-leverage themselves. Everyone is into repeat business, build on that relationship. Ask your designer who they recommend for the job. They will recommend someone that will fit your needs and, more importantly, your personality.

What strategy should you have in place for your brand's web development? I say, know your business. What I mean by that is understand your core products and or service. A business website, for selling, should be direct to the point. If you are selling ice cream, space heaters should not appear anywhere on the site. You will confuse your audience, which directly impacts your bottom line. The train of thought is when you visit the website, how fast can I get the consumer to buy my product or service? The rule of thumb is under three clicks or less. I say that so you can be aware of some of the basic principles.

Do a search and familiarize yourself with the best website practices. Also, remember your developer will give you a rundown of the most effective way to build a website. Listen to him or her, but always double-check. Business is business. If you do not know anything about the process of web development, you are in a deficient position. You must be in the ballpark of understanding why a developer makes certain design decisions. A working knowledge of what is going on is important to your process and outcomes.

Preparing for the Development

What should you have prepared for your web developer to begin the process? Let's start with an about description written and edited. Pictures of the business, inside and out. Specifications and multiple images of any products or services being sold. The hours of operation if attached to a brick and mortar location. Clear and precise contact details. Would you like the customer to email, call, or text to contact you? If required, any legalities that need to be on the website. For example, terms and conditions and or privacy statements.

If your goal is to sell products online, mention that in the beginning. E-commerce plays a big part in the development of your business. Saying it upfront can be best for all parties involved. If you are selling a service, you should have the online booking sorted before starting on the web development or design.

These are the basics of a great website. An about page, a list of services and or products, a booking experience (if available), and last but not least, a contact page. From this point, your developer would take care of the rest. The developer will contact the designer for anything graphical that is needed. The designer has your logo and will make everything fall in line with your brand's message. This is called working in harmony. Your developer will present a fully functional website built around the details of your brand. They will recommend maps, mailing lists, and landing pages to best fit your needs. That is their job. Delegating these tasks will allow you to invest more time in building your brand. Let the experts do their job. If you feel like your developer is not up to par, circle back to the strategies listed in the team chapter of this book.

This may sound harsh but agonizing over things you are not an expert in can negatively impact your business. Even looking at it from a consumer's point of view, you are biased.

My final strategy for this chapter is assembling a beta test group of three to five people. You must respect their opinion and value their input. Have them evaluate the website, take their views, and compare them to your notes. The consensus is what you will be relaying to your developer. Following these guidelines will result in a useful website that is an asset for your brand and will facilitate growth. Scalability will be the cherry on top of using a professional developer.

Chapter 9: The Optimization Memorandum

I started this book as a speech I was going to give. A number of bullet points began to flow out of me. As I continued, I wrote more and more. What resulted is information presented without the barriers we may assume.

Optimization is a term that refers to changing and innovating your business for optimum return and optimum performance. It is based on information. Once you have the information, you understand what you must do and why it must be done in a certain order.

Collateral benefits include effectiveness, speed, and usability. Effectiveness is seen in the number of people you engage. You can count the number of appointments booked per week or products sold per month. Sales result in more revenue and sustainability of your business. Speed makes it less likely that a buyer will change their mind. Click, select your barber. Click select your style. Click, select your date. And you are done—simple, and every click points toward your purpose for being on the site. Usability is about ease but also organization. When it is not done properly, you create more questions in the mind of the user. The less strain and fewer questions you create, the better.

Connection with guests is shown through caring. You must show your appreciation for your guests or customers in active ways. This is what builds the relationship. They begin to speak of you with possessive terms, "My barber. My doctor. My lash provider." We sometimes have to cancel a whole day of appointments, but we don't lose customers because of these setbacks. We communicate our difficulties and options to fix them. Our customers respond to this, but also to the relationship we have built over time by remembering birthdays, familiar conversations, and the experience we provide each time they visit.

Consider the following set of Truths:

- Customer experience is the byproduct when intangibles are delivered.
- Intangibles are the impressions based on interactions resulting from your business operations.
- Optimization includes careful attention to intangibles tracing from operations to interactions and intended impressions.

- Optimization supports referrals as impressions are shared by word of mouth and cross into digital platforms.

- Growth is a typical goal, but tracking referrals allows you to map their impressions, manage your interactions, and innovate your operations.

- A more sustainable goal is to understand why things are happening.

The first step is to optimize your verbiage across all platforms. This is where a copyrighter comes into play. Copywriting is defined as the art of rearranging words to make things sell better. For me, this solidifies the always-be-selling type of mentality. It has proven to be the most productive mindset I have embraced. That is because every point of contact is an opportunity to make a sale. Whether you are selling a service, a product, or your time. Every point of contact matters. From an Instagram bio to about sections, down to product descriptions. Every point of contact should have optimized verbiage.

I am of the school of thought that delegation creates more time to work on the business instead of at the business. That does not mean I do not accomplish a lot of those things on my own. That also does not mean that I just try to figure it out and pray for the best. When you see me execute anything on my own, it is because I first hired the professionals to do the job. I then learned from them, and when I was confident in my abilities, I took over the roles that were of interest to me.

Copywriting should always be deferred onto professionals that do it for a living. Your success will be symbiotic with their progress. I personally do not have the experience to make an impact in this area. What I do is write everything to the best of my ability. I then pass on the content to a copywriter because, at this point, there is simply too much that can go wrong. In my experiences, verbiage can turn away a demographic without even knowing. Even though my words are impactful, they can cause damage. Those well-intentioned words happen to not be methodically crafted to target an audience. That is extremely difficult to do without alienating any given demographic.

What you write can be impactful to the wrong audience. Your words can also be insignificant to the right audience. I am for taking risks, but my livelihood is not something that I play with. For these reasons, I cement copywriting as one of the pillars used for scalability and maximizing profits. Just be conscious of the fact that an optimized copy is not a one-time thing. Be aware that the times will forever be evolving. The only thing constant in life is change. To stay relevant, I refresh the business copy once per year.

Web SEO

The next area of optimization is SEO. The widely used acronym stands for Search Engine Optimization. It is defined as the science of making web pages attractive to search engines. In laymen's terms, if done correctly, your webpage will appear higher in the results of a search engine. The thought process is that clients are more likely to click on the first page of said results. Frankly, who would scroll through multiple pages? Prime real estate is the top five in any search. Aim for that type of relevance. A properly optimized website is listed on the first page. That is defined as prime real estate for search engines. A funnel for traffic. That traffic will supplement and eventually catapult the business income.

SEO, like copywriting, seems very easy on the surface. It appears to be simple enough that anyone can do it. And with the help of programs like Yoast SEO, certain levels of accomplishments can be obtained. But like copywriting, the rules and ever-changing algorithms separate the professionals from those just trying to get by.

I recommend delegating to a professional. Lean on your tribe, ask around and work with a specialist within your budget. If you would like to do it on your own, just take the necessary precautions not to hurt your business when you intend to grow its revenue.

Lastly, you want your website to load rather quickly. Think about the last time you waited on a website to load for more than 5 seconds. Then think about how much interest you lose while you wait. Finally, think about the picture that it paints while you are waiting. Would you be comfortable providing your credit card details to a website that doesn't load at a professional speed?

Luckily for you, this can be resolved rather quickly. Website speeds can be dramatically increased by running your DNS through a CDN. I know, I know. DNS stands for Domain Name System and is the phonebook of the Internet. It connects web browsers with websites. CDN stands for Content Delivery Network and is a system of distributed servers. CDN delivers pages and other web content to a user based on geographic locations, the origin of the webpage, and the content delivery server. What all this means is that your website will load a lot faster using a CDN rather than not. Ask your developer, which CDN they recommend, and if they can run your DNS through it. This is a one-time setup and will have endless benefits.

I have personally used Cloudflare for years. It has been scalable as my needs increased. I went from the free to the paid version, which was not activated at the launch of the website. It was activated as my traffic has grown in size. As my demands in bandwidth grew, I reacted by increasing the capacity—growth in terms of relevancy.

Charging a Premium

You can charge based on the extent to which you create an optimal and quality experience. A commodity must bow to the market. An experience can provide something more and charge for it.

You must first separate yourself from the market if you want to charge a premium. This will require some research. Your target audience and their environment are critical. You get to choose the population to a large extent. You must also know whether this market exists in the area you are targeting.

My barbershop business targets well-informed, affluent clientele. The experience they are used to must be replicated in my shop. Luxury is also accessibility. Most people think that it is only price. Just because something costs more does not necessarily translate into luxury experience. It is a balancing act, but you hold the cards.

I have numerous awards for being the best barber. I was there at one point. I thought that clients were most impressed by the quality of the haircut. But the more important consideration is whether the product is accessible to others. Those who pay a premium want to separate themselves from the masses. It is not about standing out. It is about accessing an experience that is beyond the norm. The balance is that the experience you create must match and exceed their expectations.

Chapter 10: The Marketing Strategy

Marketing is the understanding of your customers from all aspects. It is getting in front of people. The better the understanding, the higher your chances for loyal and repeat business. When you pair that understanding with an authentic brand representation, your business' value will be in a class of its own.

Let's take a walk.

Relationship Marketing

Marketing is defined by the activities a company undertakes to promote the buying or selling of a product or service. Breaking that definition down, we begin to understand all the variables affecting the outcome of a marketing campaign. History teaches us to focus on the variables we can control. Having a forever student mentality, I will reiterate the same notion. The key takeaway of this chapter is to hyper-focus on the variables that we can directly influence. With that said, authenticity holds the most weight in any campaign. The more an audience can relate, the better. The more honest you are, the more traction you will be able to create. Methods like email marketing, mailers, and billboards were useful during the "good ole' days." In modern times I suggest focusing on SMS marketing, social media, and geo-targeted campaigns via beacons.

Let's begin with engagement. By now, your customers are aware of your services and or products. How do they engage? Or a better question is, how should you engage them? My clientele pay upwards of $100 for an haircut. Their daily lives are completely different from the $25 haircut audience. An additional question is about connecting your product or service to their lifestyle. It makes more sense for me to sponsor a booth at a golf tournament more than spending the same amount of money on a commercial or billboard.

Of course, this is the moment when you can build a relationship anchored in trust. With proper engagement tools, your goal is to solidify the customer-business relationship. If I offer free facials at my booth at the golf tournament, I can solidify some relationships through engagement. You take the chance to showcase your personality and the experience you provide. Nothing more. Nothing less. The opportunity is not about sales or locking them in. You provide the information and allow them to make the decision for themselves.

Ongoing Engagement

A subscription model is useful for proper engagement. The last thing you want to do is communicate with an audience that did agree to be contacted. In the social media world, this is achieved rather easily. You see a comment, you respond. For SMS marketing, it is not that simple. Some laws may prevent you from making contact. You will need a form where the customer can approve future messages.

Done correctly, SMS engagement is directly tied to sales. You don't want to bombard people with content, but you want to connect with their why and their important events. The central point should be about information. This is your foundation upon which to build the relationship. Your products or services are tools for addressing the needs of the client.

For the barbershop, that is in our terms and conditions. If you make an appointment with us, you agree to open communication channels. If you are not in the service industry, a pop up can be created to run when a customer visits your website. If a guest is coming to me for a haircut, they should go nowhere else for other products like shampoo, conditioner, pomade, and other items that fit both the needs of the business and the needs of the client. The quality of product that I connect must be to the same level as the premium of the haircut. I will not sell a $10 product along with a $100 haircut. While on this subject of consistent experience, I would not offer free water or beverage services that are $10 or fountain drinks. We offer premium liquor and other amenities that fit our brand and our premium price point.

Conversion and Metrics

You must know what, where, why, and who. Know your messages and their responses. Know where your advertising is showing up, both your intentions and where it finally lands. Know why people are responding based on how you constructed your ad, and the quirks for the market that responds. Know who your customers are—both your target generally and a deeper understanding of their profile, including desires, aspirations, and sense of comfort. Knowing your data is critical to your innovation and sustainability. Understand that data is the benefit of operations even beyond the profit motive. Data can tell you what to change into even when your initial approach does not yield the desired results.

Ignorance about your data is the worst-case scenario. When your data shows trends, seasonal patterns, or responses to marketing campaigns, you want to capitalize on that information. Learn how to collect and analyze your metrics. Trends are used to capitalize on upswings. Those same trends can be used to analyze, anticipate, and mitigate loss.

The next component is converting those customers from engagement campaigns. Slow and steady will win the race. And when you think of race, think of it in terms of marathons. Build on trust. Get the customer to try your product with little to no commitment. Show the value, prove the need and the worth. Slowly transition the customer from an inquiry to buying into the brand's message.

Make this transition properly, and you will have a loyal customer who contributes repeat business to your brand. Your job is to use marketing to excite the customer. Your service and or product must add absolute value to the customer's experience. No value means no growth. The more impactful the experience, the more that customer will be back to repeat business.

Once your customers are excited, you can begin to leverage that relationship. Referrals are the single more impactful compliment a customer can provide to your business. Leveraging that existent excitement into a recommendation is a skill that must be mastered sooner than later. You want to make your customer tell all their friends about how great the product or service is. That is what we call a walking billboard. No one can advertise your business the way a satisfied customer can.

This feat is not accomplished by asking. This is where you have to practice what you preach. This is where authenticity is going to hold the most weight. Being honest with your intentions and messaging will create an environment of trust. With that environment in place, the customer will feel like they have to do their part to spread the word. Take care of the customer, and they will take care of you. Represent your brand with integrity and commitment to excellence. Your customers will appreciate it. The customer will be able to relate, which creates a sense of ownership. The next natural step is to help with the growth of the brand.

Getting the customer to that mindset will take practice and patience. A ton of data and follow through. Pay attention to the details. Commit to excellence, and everything else will follow.

SELF BALANCE

Chapter 11: Getting Balanced

No matter how you explain it, no matter how many YouTube videos you watch, no matter how many Ted Talks you listen to, balance is within you. You must learn to listen to yourself because everyone experiences balance differently. You must listen to your inner voice; what you like and what you don't like. We don't listen to our thoughts about enjoyment. You may like to jog or travel or sit still.

I have clients who sit in my chair and are still working. They act as if they will fall apart if they stop working. I have other clients that will put the world on freeze and their phone on silent for their haircut. I find that those that beat themselves up do not smell the roses until it is too late. A well-off client does not think that they have enough time in the day. Anxiety and alopecia come with the territory. A billionaire client pauses everything. I used to think that the billionaire afforded or earned that experience. I found that this was not true. There is a difference between the two individuals. The difference is that the billionaire has mastered the art of being present at each moment. You must truly be present to achieve your reward. You must truly know yourself to achieve balance.

Knowing Yourself

When you are truly in a place of understanding who you are, it is a different ballgame. Nothing else is relevant. Early on, you are doing things because that is what society tells you will get you success and wealth. People confuse wealth with freedom. They want money so they can go on vacation whenever they want. They are using the tool to get freedom. Once you get there, you will only do what you want to do. The degree of attention will be different because you are 100% involved.

I started golfing two weeks ago with my buddy. He went twice since then. I went every day. When we went together again, it looked like I had been golfing for years compared to him. I had more of an interest when compared to him. I treat it like physical chess. I am taking the time to photograph my swing. My friend, on the other hand, is checking his phone. He is not as interested.

Once you have the freedom, even without the wealth, you will find a level of balance that is beyond financial. When the wealth arrives, you are ready with the mental part of the experience. You will look at everything completely differently. The intensity that you put into those things that you choose will yield greater results when compared to others. Your focus and your interest make the difference.

We get into a mindset that equates to illusions of grandeur. For example, some look at the clothes you wear, the car you drive, or the house you live in and judge who you are. We put on those airs and look in the mirror and do not recognize who we are. When you find your Zen, you stop caring about the pretense of wealth. You begin to look at the experience of freedom. I remember when I had an Audi sedan and SUV, I traded both of them in and paid cash for a reliable car. I look at those who struggle with their car payments and remember that I don't have those stressors anymore.

I had a client that was like a father figure. He parked right in front. He wanted to show me something and asked, "Would you walk me in next time I had an appointment." I walked down to meet him. He parked right in front. He made sure to allow me to see him get out of his car. He was the type to speak without speaking. He looked over at my car. He knew it was mine. He nodded to me, and I knew exactly the lesson he was teaching me at that moment. The light switch went on.

"What am I doing? Who am I trying to impress? I have a wife and a child. This man is a billionaire and does not need a car to tell him who he is." It was a regular moment for that mentor. It was a life-changing moment for me. I began to see my choices differently. You do not need objects to validate your success. You don't need a physical representation. As Jay-Z says in 4:44, "Y'all on the 'gram holdin' money to your ear. There's a disconnect; we don't call that money over here." Some want you to believe they have money. But money is just the tool. Freedom is the goal.

Even the Hermes belt is not meant to be shown. It is a tool for negotiation. When you open your suit coat for negotiation, your collaborator knows where the negotiations begin because they see your belt as you sit down.

Being Present

Being present is being in the moment. You are not living more than one moment at once. You forget about everything outside the moment you are in. Many cannot say that they are practiced with that. When you are looking at Instagram while spending time with your kids, you are not 100% there with your children.

You know about your contributions to the present long afterward. You are giving someone the gift of time, but you may not find the reward right away. If you are doing it right, it comes later. Compare a scenario where your children say, "I wish we had spent more time together." If you did it right and your children say, "I'm glad we did that as a family." Consider the type of person your daughter grows up to be when you give your presence and engagement rather than fake love.

Being present is not learning; it is discipline. You must discipline yourself to say that nothing else matters in this moment. You must cultivate quality time. People think that it is about large quantities of time. It could be 5 minutes. You know how good my daughter feels when we are talking, and the phone rings and I refuse to pick it up? She is cool. She says, "It's okay, Dad. I know it's work."

"No. You are the most important person to me at the moment." My children still remind me of a time when we went to a park. They remember it like it was hours. It was only for 5 minutes.

Customer Relationship Management

When you go above and beyond, and they find you because of strategy and stay because of relationship, something else happens. It's magical. Your stories become intertwined. When you take the guidance from this book, you get that relationship opportunity. Everyone has a different capacity. Your clients are going to look out for you and your interests because of the relationship. Every client will offer you something different because of the relationships. You are in a position to learn without malicious intent from a wide range of people.

When you go to college, you learn from one person at a time. When you enter into your business relationship, that experience is multiplied times 100. That value is intangible. You can follow textbooks and not find the solution and opportunity. You find an expanded experience with relationships. The potential is unmatched.

The best advice I can give you is to genuinely care. When you care, you will remember the wife's name, the birthday, the anniversary. You also augment the systems that work for that. We use a system within our booking system for keeping notes related to each client. We care enough to find those systems that work for our uses and the connection we desire with our guests.

Section Case Study

If you have 500 clients in your book and it takes one minute on average to send messages. That's 500 minutes. If you do that 3 times per week, you are committing 1500 minutes to one task that supports but does not make you money in your business. That is 25 hours that must be calculated against what your best performing service could be making if the time was used offering that service. The challenge with this time transfer does not stop with the financial drain. Recognize that the need for this action does not cease once it is completed for one client. The more clients you gain, the more time is potentially spent on this function of your business. You limit your growth because the number of hours in the day are finite. Even hiring additional staff will reach a financial and logistic breaking point. When I talk about saving time, that is exactly what I mean. And that is just intentional messages sent to clients. That does not include follow-up, rescheduling, prompting, reminders, and social media.

Enter our solution for balance across multiple considerations of business and life spaces. St-Ble asks you to set the parameters. From there, it takes care of the grunt work for you. Over the course of the month, you reclaim hours that were previously lost as well as enhancing the experience for your customers. You have less unexpected losses and more pleasant gains.

If you are working at your business, you don't have time to work on your business. This is a common saying. The power of great tools is to get back to working on your business. Reclaiming that time to think about the business allows you to create new models and make the business better. The balance is the most important currency you gain. You cannot work on your business all day. Business cannot be everything. But the beast of a business that provides monster profits must be fed with time and energy. You can feed the beast, reap the profits, and maintain the balance made possible by tools like St-Ble.

Spending time with your family will return value exponentially. It will be much more rewarding to return to work after time away with your family. Think of yourself as a battery. When you are present with your family, you get the recharge that you need. It is not healthy to spend time at the job repeatedly without recharging yourself. You will eventually hate the business that you invested time in building. On the flip side, if you reclaim quality time and apply it to appropriately recharging, every return to the business is a return from vacation. You will enjoy the time at work more and realize a boost in productivity. Your mind will be freed from the daily grind to conceptualize innovations and respond to opportunities. You set your business on a solid foundation. That means that you can take additional risks with great potential rewards.

Chapter 12: Maintaining Balance

If you do not take care of your body, you are not balanced. At some point, your body will let you down. You may be curious about how long you will live and what you can accomplish in that time. But if you are not taking care of your health, the answers are difficult to obtain. The gain will be tenuous. And you will not be as capable of maintaining the gains you do accomplish.

Maintain an understanding about how your body works. This is critical to your health and wellbeing. Your body requires water, sunlight, air, exercise, and food for optimal functioning. It is fair to say that many people take these for granted or refuse to bother with them at all. For example, I am always amazed when I find that people do not drink an adequate amount of water. Vitality, metabolism, mental clarity, waste elimination, and physical functioning are all tied to this simple ingestible compound. It is abundant and accessible for many of us. Yet many forego its benefits to their peril. Beyond the basics, you have a myriad of options for how to translate activity into physical and mental health. Some enjoy running. Others enjoy swimming. I just started golfing. It is a community-type game that offers relaxing socialization. It also fits my networking needs and allows me to engage in a comfortable environment. It has elements that keep both the body and the mind stimulated.

Deeper Understanding

Understand that time is a precious resource. Time is the most powerful yet most fragile resource in the world. Most of it is mismanaged in any one day. Other times, we wear ourselves out in excess and end up taking time to recuperate. Once you understand that fragility, you will look at time differently. Each moment is valuable for recreation, productivity, or engagement. Recreation is first because each of us needs to find peace and tranquility in life as much as possible. This sets the proper stage for other experiences. Productivity is the work you do. It is not just a chore or completion of a to-do list. Healthy work provides mental benefits, including pride in a job well done, and learning that may be applied to later tasks. Engagement brings our attention back to the importance of relationships. People, especially supportive people and those engaged when you are doing what you love, energize you emotionally. Life is challenging, but engagement brings purpose.

That is why it is so important to be present in each moment. You do not get those moments back after they are gone. If you complete a job with less vigor and professionalism than you are capable of, you do not get a chance to redo that moment. You may have a chance to do better on the next opportunity if you get a next time. Your choice of recreation, production, and engagement matters. It is possible to enjoy your time, learn, and collaborate at the same time. Your approach to people also matters. This includes attention to insults and negativity. If you waste your moments with negative attitudes, you lose those moments. Everything you approach in life will dramatically change when you realize this.

All this balance leads to a deeper understanding of the purpose of your business endeavor. Your goal is freedom. The byproduct of freedom is money. Consider money a relative commodity. You only need it for your sustenance. That means that you do not need all the money. You only need what is required to achieve the lifestyle that you desire. Freedom to live that life in your specific reality of abundance is what we all strive for.

Freedom is incompatible with greed and waste. If people did not waste, we would have enough resources for six earths. As it is, we are in a perpetual deficit of resources. A restaurant in the US will offer you free bread or chips when you sit down. That is a luxury that costs in other countries. We are already resource-rich just by living in the United States. When you understand this, you realize that freedom and happiness are separate from money, progress, and success. You learn how to recognize your priorities and achieve what really matters. You also grow beyond the need to impress people with money. You develop beyond the pretense and the inclination to look like a million bucks before you have a million bucks. When you are free, the money comes. Chase the freedom rather than chasing the money.

Mind & Body and Family

Scheduling time is your first step. Intentionally spend the time on what you know will develop toward your goals. My approach to my daily life is a priority list. I review what tasks I have, the priority or insistence of any one task, the time I have, and the energy I have available. I am much more intentional about the time I allot to even my important activities. My goal is to maximize the time, not just use it. We all have the same 24 hours in a day. You may have challenges that I do not have. I may have limitations that you are not familiar with. But each of us has time to build, to overcome, and to grow. The most successful people are always sharpening their minds. They say that the most successful people read a book a week. They have a hunger for knowledge that is insatiable. When they need to pull a trigger, they have the information to make an informed decision.

I promote the idea that the solutions extend from you. That is why a sharp mind is so important. It has been said that you have everything you need to be successful. A sharp mind recognizes capacity, capability, and opportunity. Capacity is the ability to clear the mental, emotional, and physical space for change and growth to occur. Capability is the know-how to develop a plan of action that fits capacity. Opportunity is the component describing a chance to implement the plan. Each of these must be understood in the context of solid information.

For example, a person may say that they will start a social media platform because people are tired of using Facebook. That statement comes out of ignorance. You may not know that Facebook spends hundreds of thousands of dollars on search engine optimization (SEO) per month to drive traffic to their servers. Your hope to take down Facebook must be more than a passing note about what some of your friends are opting to do.

Some may say they will be the next Coca-Cola. You may not know the growth and development strategy in the food and beverage sector. You may have no clue of the relationships that the company has built with community functions, venues, and food chains. It is not a question of simple drive and ideas; it is a question of your ability to compete in the market.

The catch-22 is that you must not lose the "I can do anything I put my mind to." But that feeling cannot come from ignorance. You can compete. You can be the WhatsApp or Instagram to Facebook. You could be the company that innovates to meet a need that has not been addressed. Just make sure that you lead with research and solid information. You must pair that with market knowledge and market research. You see the barriers, opportunities, strengths, and threats differently. This is a question of time savings. Spend your time with what has a greater potential to work rather than giving time (wasting time) on ideas that are poorly informed.

Before you vocalize your idea, consider your audience. Your ideas are currency, but they are not necessarily transferrable. Once you process and reach a point where you have no additional reasons it will not work, you are in a good position. Develop your idea until you find no reason it will not work. It is time then to put money behind the idea.

Delayed gratitude is the best gratitude. I don't care what job you are working. You do not work that job 24 hours per day. On average, a shift for work is 8-10 hours. You sleep for a solid 8 hours. That is 18 hours. What are you doing with the remaining 6 hours? Even with an hour commute both ways, you still have 4 hours. The challenge is that people want instant gratification. They want something to materialize now. They want to enjoy television, get more sleep, or something else instead of pursuing their dreams. If you delay that gratification and work toward your dreams, your success will come sooner, and you will enjoy it more.

You have immediate family and everyone else. Family or not, you must surround yourself with the right people. They will not pull you down necessarily, but they will hinder your progress. It will help to limit those interactions that waste time.

Your immediate family helps you to focus on what is important long-term. If you breakdown what you are doing when engaging with them, you begin to realize that there are takeaways that are valuable for business. Not only are there lessons that translate like patience, perseverance, camaraderie, and genuine caring, there are revelations about your own tolerance, vision, and opportunity.

With family, you must find an interest point that keeps your energy up. Doing activities together is better when you are excited about them. You may do something others like for a moment, but you will put more in and benefit more from something that you are interested in.

Learning

Remember to continue to learn and grow. It does not necessarily need to be new things. Yet there are so many ways to take in information these days. Audio books, podcasts, books, TedTalks, and more are available. The more information you get, the more you understand how little you know. Stay hungry. Continue in development and practice. Rehearse your mental acuity, curiosity, and chemistry.

The sports figures who become professionals all have natural talent. The difference between an elite athlete who plays above the field of players is that they continue to practice and learn.

Others do not put in the time on their craft, often choosing to engage in instant gratification instead.

The easiest way to do this is to start. There is not a special tutorial. Just go to a search engine and type in "How to do X." There is no secret. No one can put in the work for you. If you expect someone to put in the work, it will not end well. If you put in the work, you will find that it is all you need.

Conclusion

Thank you for taking the time to read my book. It means more than you could ever know. My hope is that Strategies & Relationships inspire you to take that first step and begin your journey on firm ground. "Here's to the crazy ones, ..., the rebels, ..., the round pegs in the square holes... the ones who see things differently..." You know have all the tools needed to make a difference. Share your journey and keep me informed. I would love to hear from you.

relationships@intlsosa.com

Resources

My website:

intlsosa.com

Keep up to date with all things Sosa.

Business blog:

Ledgr.xyz

A growth mindset. Opinions, thoughts, and ideas curated to elevate your business. Created by /mercantes & friends, est. 2020

St-ble Communications:

St-ble.com

Think, "you'll never go back," type of different. St-ble replaces third-party communications and social media messengers with 1-on-1 direct contact.

The Limited Availability Podcast:

A podcast about the mentality needed to go from good to great.

E-mail:

relationships@intlsosa.com

Telephone:

+1.646.970.8870

Social Media:

@intlsosa